98-742

Nichols, John
    The history of the Marlins

F
L
O
R
I
D
A

J O H N   N I C H O L S

THE HISTORY OF THE

MARLINS

C R E A T I V E   E D U C A T I O N

Published by Creative Education
123 South Broad Street, Mankato, Minnesota 56001
Creative Education is an imprint of The Creative Company

Designed by Rita Marshall

Photos by: Allsport Photography, Focus on Sports, SportsChrome.

Library of Congress Cataloging-in-Publication Data

Nichols, John, 1966–
The History of the Florida Marlins / by John Nichols.
p. cm. — (Baseball)
Summary: Highlights the history of the Florida Marlins, the major league
baseball expansion team that came to play in Miami in 1993.
ISBN: 0-88682-909-7

1. Florida Marlins (Baseball team)—History—Juvenile literature.
[1. Florida Marlins (Baseball team)—History. 2. Baseball—History.]
I. Title. II. Series: Baseball (Mankato, Minn.)

GV875.F56N53 1999
796.357'64'097593—dc21   97-46396

First edition

9 8 7 6 5 4 3 2 1

With its warm sun, beautiful beaches, and brilliant blue ocean, Miami, Florida, has been attracting tourists and vacationers for some time. The area's first European visitor was Spanish explorer Ponce de Leon in 1513. He was so taken with the tropical paradise that he believed he had discovered the Fountain of Youth, a mythical place that promised the aged could become young again by merely drinking the healing waters.

As it turned out, Ponce de Leon was somewhat right to search for the legendary fountain in Florida. Although Florida can't ever promise eternal youth, today thousands of

First baseman Orestes Destrade.

Americans retire each year to South Florida to enjoy comfort and relaxation, escaping harsh northern winters to bask in warm weather year-round.

One of Florida's more frequent visitors over the years has been major league baseball. For decades the state has provided the ideal atmosphere for big-league teams to shake off the dust of the off-season and begin each year anew with spring training.

Every March, the game's arms, legs, and minds would come to be exercised and strengthened under the warm Florida sun, but each April, the teams would pack up and leave to begin the regular season in their northern homes. Finally, in 1993, the fans of South Florida were given a team of their own—the Florida Marlins, based in Miami.

The Marlins, like most expansion teams, weren't very good early on, but they quickly became one of baseball's finest ballclubs. Star former players such as outfielder Gary Sheffield and catcher Charles Johnson, along with pitcher Livan Hernandez, transformed the Marlins from a struggling expansion team to a World Series champion in the span of just five years.

1 9 9 1

The Marlins, named for a minor-league team of the '50s, unveiled their team logo on July 5.

MARLINS MADE FROM SCRATCH

For H. Wayne Huizenga, July 5, 1991, was a happy day. His five-year dream came true. Huizenga, the owner of the Blockbuster Video store franchise, was granted ownership of a major league baseball team.

Huizenga's Florida Marlins were born that day, and while the new owner felt great excitement, he also felt a new

Former Marlin Bobby Bonilla powered the '97 champs.

sense of responsibility. "We had worked so hard in getting South Florida a baseball team," explained Huizenga. "And when it happened, I was thrilled for a moment, but then I realized that our job wasn't over. It had just begun."

Huizenga was right. Building a ballclub that Florida's baseball-starved fans could be proud of would be the big challenge for the franchise's front office, and unfortunately, its options were limited. Most of the Marlins' first roster would consist of players selected from the special 1992 expansion draft. The draft was to provide a pool of talent for the Marlins and their fellow expansion team, the Colorado Rockies. But as newly named Marlins manager Rene Lachemann would quip, "It's a pool all right, but it ain't very deep." All of the players available in the draft were there because they were either inexperienced young players or were aging veterans, or their previous big-league clubs had given up on them.

Florida's long-term plan was to choose younger players, then try to develop them over time. Winning a lot of games the first year was not expected, nor was it a high priority. South Florida's fans understood the pains of expansion baseball and backed the team to the tune of 3,064,847 spectators in 1993. What they were treated to was the rise of one new star and the final flash of brilliance from another.

A "BARBARIAN" STARS WITH "LIGHTS OUT" HARVEY

The Marlins' first season was a classic example of expansion baseball—there were few wins and many long stretches of losing. Nevertheless, the South Florida fans were treated to many thrills during the course of a 64-win season. Two players in particular dominated the '93 Marlins' high-lights: outfielder Jeff Conine and closer Bryan Harvey. Co-nine and Harvey were both expansion-draft selections who found themselves in Florida at completely different stages of their careers.

Conine had started out as a highly touted prospect of the Kansas City Royals. At 6-foot-2 and 220 pounds, the out-fielder put up productive numbers for five seasons in the Royals' farm system, but never was able to stick with the big club. "The Royals had a solid, veteran outfield, and they just didn't have room to carry an inexperienced kid like me," said Conine. "I thought I'd never get a real chance." Luckily, the Marlins knew all about the Tacoma, Washington, native and took him with the 22nd pick in the expansion draft.

It didn't take long for the 26-year-old rookie to begin pay-ing back the Marlins for their confidence in him. In Florida's first-ever regular-season game, Conine went 4-for-4, scored two runs, and stole a base as the Marlins defeated the Los Angeles Dodgers 6–3.

Conine went on to hit .292, rap 174 hits, and drive in 79 runs for the season, finishing third in the '93 National League Rookie of the Year race. But more importantly, Florida fans had found a hero with whom they could identify. The per-sonable Conine was an immediate fan favorite—so much so that the muscular yet mild-mannered outfielder was tagged with the nickname "Conine the Barbarian," a reference to the fictional muscle-bound character of comic books and movies, Conan the Barbarian. "Jeff may not have the guns [arm muscles] of the real Conan, but he sure played big for

Benito Santiago belted the Marlins' first-ever home run, a two-run shot against San Fran-cisco on April 12.

Closer Bryan Harvey was one of the Marlins' first stars.

Knuckleball specialist, pitcher Charlie Hough.   11

us," said Lachemann. "I hate to think where we would have been without him."

Lachemann could have said the same thing about the Marlins' other first-year standout, Bryan Harvey. Unlike Conine, Harvey had been an established star in the major leagues with the California Angels, but injuries and a large salary made him expendable. The Marlins decided to take a gamble on the hard-throwing but fragile right-hander. They knew that with Harvey's violent throwing motion and aging arm, serious injury was always a possibility. But when healthy, Harvey had a hard fastball and devastating split-finger that made him nearly unhittable. "When Harv is feeling it, that splitter just explodes downward. You can't hit it, and you can't lay off it," explained Marlins teammate Dave Magadan. "When he's got that going in the ninth inning, it's lights out for the other team."

In 1993, Harvey had a season for the ages, saving 45 of the Marlins' 64 wins, striking out 73 batters in 69 innings, and posting a minuscule 1.70 ERA. "Considering the ballclub he was pitching for, that may have been one of the best performances by a closer I've ever seen," gushed awestruck Los Angeles Dodgers manager Tommy Lasorda. But unfortunately, the brilliant season would take its toll on Harvey's talented but injury-prone arm. During the following spring training, Harvey began to suffer severe pain in his elbow. He underwent surgery and made several attempts to come back, but Harvey would never regain the form that made him unhittable in 1993. "That was sad," remarked Lachemann. "The guy pitched his heart out for us. I just hope, no matter what

1 9 9 3

Gary Sheffield belted a home run in the Marlins' first-ever All-Star Game at-bat July 13.

the future holds, that Florida fans remember how great he was that year."

SHEFFIELD BRINGS BIG BAT BACK HOME

Despite their losing record and expansion status, the Marlins quickly discovered they had a definite advantage over other teams in attracting star talent. The state of Florida is a renowned hotbed for baseball, producing many of the game's current stars. When the Marlins were born, many former and current Floridians expressed interest in moving closer to home to play for the fledgling ballclub. Midway through the 1993 season, Tampa, Florida, native Gary Sheffield got his wish. The slugging outfielder/third baseman was acquired by the Marlins in a six-player trade that brought much-needed power to the middle of the Florida lineup. "I'm here to help this team win," said a smiling Sheffield. "I feel very fortunate to be home in front of family and friends."

Pitcher Chris Hammond finished the Marlins' first season as the team's winningest pitcher with 11 victories.

Sheffield's career started in Milwaukee in 1988. The Brewers had slotted the young phenom to replace aging Hall of Fame shortstop Robin Yount, who had been moved to the outfield. Sheffield had all the tools—a lightning-quick bat, powerful arm, and above-average speed—but being a 19-year-old major-leaguer proved to be too much to handle. "I was a kid far from home, and I was miserable," explained Sheffield. "The Brewers had a lot of expectations for me, and it was just too much. I had a lot of problems."

After a series of disappointing, injury-filled seasons in Mil-

Infielder Bret Barberie posted a .301 batting average to boost Florida's attack at the plate.

waukee, Sheffield was traded to the San Diego Padres before the 1992 campaign. The new city and a move to third base proved to be just the tonic for Sheffield's game. He exploded for 33 homers, 100 RBIs, and a .330 batting average—good enough to land him the National League batting title. Unfortunately, the financially strapped Padres could not afford to carry Sheffield's contract. The team approached the blossoming star early in the '93 season and asked if he had a preference in where he would like to be dealt. Sheffield responded immediately, "Send me home."

With Sheffield in the lineup, the Marlins' offense commanded respect. "Gary's just a physical freak of nature," noted his former Padres teammate Fred McGriff. "When he swings, his bat is so fast, it's just a blur. With reflexes like that, the pitch must look like a beach ball. It's unfair."

During the strike-shortened 1994 season, Sheffield treated many pitchers unfairly, pounding out 27 homers, driving in 78 runs, and hitting .276 in only 322 at-bats. Those numbers—combined with Conine's .319 average, 18 homers, and 82 RBIs—drove the Marlins' offense to new heights. But just as Florida seemed poised to become a .500 team, the players' strike ended the season after 115 games. The Marlins' record was frozen at 51–64.

"We weren't going to win any pennants," grumbled Sheffield, "but I wish we could have had the chance to reach .500. That would have been a big step for a second-year club."

Still, the Marlins seemed to be a team on the rise, and there was more help on the way. A young catcher by the name of Charles Johnson was called up late in 1994, and for opposing base-stealers, life would never be the same again.

Jeff Conine provided plenty of offense for the Marlins.

Talented catcher Benito Santiago.

One of the trademarks of National League baseball is raw speed. The larger NL ballparks invite players to slash the ball into the gaps and then run, rather than belt it over the fence as their American League counterparts often do. Base-stealing legends the likes of Maury Wills, Lou Brock, and Vince Coleman have taught the league's shell-shocked catchers a very important lesson over the years: speed kills.

By the mid '90s National League speedsters were stealing at an alarming rate. Around the league, catchers were considered above-average defensively if they could throw out merely one in three potential thieves. The Marlins knew that to be competitive, they would need a strong-armed catcher to neutralize the running game. So when reports began to pour in about a catcher with a cannon arm from the nearby University of Miami, the Marlins wasted no time. Charles Edward Johnson was the Marlins' 1992 first-round pick in the amateur draft.

Johnson came to the organization with an already glossy résumé that included college All-American honors and a spot on the 1992 U.S. Olympic baseball team. But even with all the advance billing, Florida could not believe the package of talent the 6-foot-2 and 220-pound catcher brought to the field. "The first day of spring training, Charles comes in, and everybody's watching him out of the corner of their eye," laughs Conine. "And the first time he has to throw down to second, the pitch bounces about a foot and a half in front of the plate. Charles backhands it and, from his knees, fires this

Outfielder Jeff Conine was chosen to represent the Florida club at the All-Star Game.

Always hustling, Chuck Carr made the Marlins' offense go (pages 18-19).

absolute pea to second. Everybody just looked at each other and started smiling."

In his first year as the Marlins' closer, reliever Rob Nen saved 15 games for the club.

Johnson's defense gave the Marlins a lot to smile about during his rookie year in 1995. He gunned down an astronomical 42 percent of opposing runners who attempted to steal and handled the Marlins' youthful pitching staff with the patience of a veteran. Johnson's dazzling defensive performance earned him his first Gold Glove award for fielding excellence, but an added bonus was his steady offensive production. "Being that he's so young, we thought it would take awhile before Charles's offensive skills caught up with his defense," said Lachemann. "But he surprised us a little." Johnson hit a respectable .251 with 11 homers in 1995.

With the addition of Johnson, the Marlins hoped to reach

Veteran third baseman Terry Pendleton.

the .500 mark in 1995, but injuries destroyed their chances. Sheffield was limited to 63 games by a torn thumb ligament, and Johnson missed three weeks after being hit on the hand by a pitch. For Florida, the 67–76 final record was a disappointment. "But if anything, it just makes us want it more," said Sheffield. "You get knocked down. You get back up. That's baseball."

MARLINS ARE ARMED AND DANGEROUS

Former NL MVP Andre Dawson signed with the Marlins as a free agent and hit .257 for the season.

In the winter before the 1996 season, Marlins owner Wayne Huizenga decided to fast-forward his ballclub's development. Attendance at Pro Player Stadium had slipped from more than three million in 1993 to 1.7 million in 1995. The owner felt more was needed to give the Florida faithful a winner. With that in mind, Huizenga shopped baseball's free-agent market with gusto, signing starting pitchers Kevin Brown (from Baltimore) and Al Leiter (Toronto), along with fleet center fielder Devon White (Toronto), to bolster the Marlins' pitching, defense, and offensive production.

The moves paid big dividends, as White battled through nagging injuries to hit .274 with 17 homers and 84 runs batted in. The graceful outfielder also managed 22 steals while igniting the Marlins' offense from the number-two spot in the batting order.

Brown and Leiter quickly established themselves as one of the league's most devastating one-two punches on the mound. The right-handed Brown went 17–11 in spite of receiving the worst run support in the league. He captured the

The talented Moises Alou.

major-league ERA crown with a mark of 1.89 and also posted three shutouts.

Leiter went 16–12 with a 2.93 ERA and 200 strikeouts. The two hurlers anchored the young staff, and the league quickly took notice that hits and runs weren't easy to come by in Florida anymore. "Kevin Brown's got that nasty hard sinker, and the lefty [Leiter] has serious heat," muttered Colorado Rockies slugger Dante Bichette. "Plus the lefty's about half-wild, which makes me real nervous."

Second baseman Quilvio Veras swiped 56 bases to lead the team.

Leiter made Bichette, and the rest of the Rockies, extremely nervous when on May 11, 1996, he struck out six and walked two in notching the Marlins' first-ever no-hitter in a 11–0 victory over Colorado. "After I caught him the first inning, I almost wanted to laugh," said Johnson. "He had such overpowering stuff, I almost felt sorry for those guys."

In addition to the big two of Brown and Leiter, the Marlins finally found a closer to fill the shoes of the departed Bryan Harvey. Right-hander Rob Nen posted 35 saves, a 1.95 ERA, and 92 strikeouts in 83 innings during 1996.

On the offensive side, Gary Sheffield and Jeff Conine combined to pile up eye-popping numbers. Sheffield thumped 42 homers and drove in 120 runs while batting .314. Conine cracked 26 homers with 95 RBIs and posted an impressive .293 average.

Unfortunately, despite all the big numbers put up by Marlins players, the team's record improved only marginally. After a break-even start, Florida began to stumble, plunging eight games under .500 by mid-July.

With his high-priced team caught in a downward spiral,

Edgar Renteria hit safely in 22 consecutive games to set the Marlins' club record.

Huizenga decided to make a change. He fired manager Rene Lachemann and replaced him with John Boles, who had served as the team's vice president of player development. Boles had never been a field manager before, but his reputation as a strong evaluator of talent and a person who believed in a disciplined approach to the game made him an easy choice. "Rene has done a lot for this team and the organization," explained a determined Boles. "But these guys are better than what they've shown, and now it's my job to get them to that level."

Under Boles' direction the Marlins showed improvement, going 40–35 down the stretch to finish the season with an 80–82 mark. Huizenga, however, was not yet satisfied. The Marlins drew 1.74 million fans in 1996, an improvement from '95, but in Huizenga's view, still a disappointment. "I feel we have yet to capture the imagination of the Florida baseball fan," he explained after the season. "We, as an organization, have to do more."

LEYLAND TAKES THE REIGNS

With the off-season return of John Boles to the front office, the Marlins set their sights on acquiring one of the most respected managers in the game: Jim Leyland.

Leyland had been the mastermind behind the powerful Pittsburgh Pirates teams of the early '90s. His ballclubs had piled up 849 wins and three division titles in his 11 seasons at the helm, but after the 1996 campaign, Leyland decided to step down. Pittsburgh, a cash-poor franchise, couldn't afford to keep the players Leyland had developed, so piece by piece, the mighty Pirates were sold off to the highest bidders. Leyland, nearing retirement, wanted one more chance to manage a team with a realistic chance to go to the World Series.

Several teams tried to secure Leyland's services, but Florida, with its warm weather, talented roster, and aggressive owner, won out. Leyland joined the Marlins October 4, 1996.

"It was a pretty simple decision, really," joked Leyland. "Mr. Huizenga told me he wants to win a championship, and I said 'I do too.' There wasn't much to negotiate after that."

Leyland's decision to pursue a World Series title with the Marlins gave the expansion franchise some championship grit to feed off of, and his new players relished the opportunity. "For those of us who've been here since the beginning, this is one exciting day," said Conine. "This team has a lot of talent, but we haven't learned to be winners yet. Leyland will show us what it takes."

1 9 9 6

Center fielder Devon White legged out 37 doubles to lead the Marlins.

MARLINS HOOK CHAMPIONSHIP

For many organizations, the addition of Jim Leyland to a talented young ballclub would have been an amazing off-season all by itself. But for the Florida Marlins, it was just the start. Within 90 days of Leyland's October signing, the Marlins also landed free-agent stars third baseman Bobby Bonilla (from Baltimore), pitcher Alex Fernandez (Chicago White Sox), and outfielder Moises Alou (Montreal).

"With these new guys I really feel strongly about our chances," said Leyland. "I think we've improved dramatically." The new manager proved to be absolutely correct as

A superb catcher, former Marlin Charles Johnson (pages 26-27).

After a midseason call-up, rookie Livan Hernandez went 9–3 with a 3.18 ERA and 72 strikeouts.

the Marlins enjoyed their finest season ever, going 92–70, finishing just behind the first-place Atlanta Braves in the NL East and capturing the National League wild-card spot. Driving the Marlins' run to the postseason were the productive performances of Alou, Kevin Brown, and Alex Fernandez.

Alou was a force in the middle of the lineup, hitting .292 with 23 home runs and 115 RBIs. Brown continued his stingy ways on the mound, going 16–8 with a 2.89 ERA and 205 strikeouts, while the left-handed Fernandez posted a 17–12 mark with a 3.59 ERA. "We didn't get a career year from anybody," said Bonilla after the season, "but a lot of guys had solid years."

The Marlins' solid year gained potent momentum when the first-time playoff team battled past their National League playoff opponents, the San Francisco Giants and the Atlanta Braves, to reach the World Series. "This is a great feeling," said first baseman Darren Daulton after clinching the National League Championship Series over the Braves. "But I think we all know now what has to be done."

The Marlins' opponent in the 1997 World Series would be the Cleveland Indians. In the first six games both teams battled desperately to gain control, but neither could; the series was deadlocked at three games apiece. Game seven quickly turned into a nervewracking affair as the Indians struck first with two runs in the top of the third inning. The Marlins threatened several times but did not break through until Bonilla's seventh-inning solo homer closed the gap to 2–1. Neither team scored in the eighth, and the Marlins were down to their last three outs in the bottom of the ninth.

"We were all pretty nervous, but we still believed we

could pull it off," said Jeff Conine. The Marlins' faith was rewarded when second baseman Craig Counsell hit a sacrifice fly to deep right field, good enough to score a tagging Alou from third base to tie the game and send it into extra innings. Neither team scored in the 10th inning, and Cleveland was blanked again in the top half of the 11th.

With the tension rising in Pro Player Stadium, the Marlins managed to load the bases in their half of the 11th with shortstop Edgar Renteria coming to the plate. Indians pitcher Charles Nagy pitched carefully to the shortstop, knowing the game and series were on the line, but Renteria fought him off and stroked a line drive over Nagy that just cleared the pitcher's outstretched glove before bouncing into center field. Counsell scored easily from third and the Marlins were World Series champions. "What a game; what a series," exclaimed Leyland. "The people of South Florida really got a taste of what the World Series and championship baseball are all about tonight." The Marlins' championship win was the first ever by a wild-card team since baseball adopted the new playoff format in 1995. "It just shows how tough this team is," said Bonilla. "Nobody gave us much of a chance, but we proved all the experts wrong."

Unfortunately for the champion Marlins, the victory party was short-lived. Soon after the series, owner Wayne Huizenga decided that he could no longer afford to carry the team's $50 million payroll, and that cuts would have to be made. Within a span of three months, Alou, Rob Nen, Brown, Devon White, Conine, Darren Daulton, and pitchers Dennis Cook and Tony Saunders were either traded, left by free agency, or lost in baseball's expansion draft held to

1 9 9 8

The Marlins were hoping to return to the World Series on the talent of young outfielder Todd Dunwoody.

29

Talented young pitcher Livan Hernandez.

The last of the original Marlins, shortstop Edgar Renteria.

1 9 9 8

Newly acquired third baseman Todd Zeile was expected to add power and leadership to the '98 Florida club.

stock baseball's two newest teams, the Arizona Diamondbacks and the Tampa Bay Devil Rays. Huizenga continued to slash the Marlins' payroll by trading away the last of his established stars—Charles Johnson, Gary Sheffield, and Bobby Bonilla—early in the 1998 season.

With all this talent lost, the Marlins would be hard-pressed to stay atop the baseball world. Although the Marlins were weakened, Florida was resting its hopes on the team's cast of young players. 1997 rookie pitching sensation Livan Hernandez gave Florida a new ace to count on in the starting rotation. Edgar Renteria, who many felt could become one of the game's best shortstops, anchored the Marlins' infield. A host of young outfielders looked to fill the shoes of the team's departed stars. And last, but not least, Leyland would be at the helm to guide the Marlins through the transition.

With a rebuilt roster, it may be some time before the Marlins ascend to the World Series throne again. A new horizon awaits the former expansion team. Leyland and his new-look Marlins now expect to add more chapters to their team's short but exciting history book.